THREE BILLY-GOATS GRUFF

flowers

nest

grass

herbs

river

meadow

water

bridge

big
Billy-goat
Gruff

second
Billy-goat
Gruff

young
Billy-goat
Gruff

Troll

hooves

houses

horns

cakes

These are illustrations of some of the characters and things from the book. Let your listeners See and Say them, get to know them, before you read the story. Then, as you read, pause and point to each picture in the text, letting the child supply the illustrated word. Young children love to follow stories in this way and it gives them a first exercise in the movement of reading.

There were once **3** goats who lived among high hills, where wild  grew and eagles had their . The **3** goats were brothers and their family name was Gruff.

The  roamed among the hills each day searching for sweet  and  to eat. And one day they came to a deep 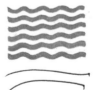. On the far side they could see a full of long juicy . "The is very deep but there is a ," said . "We must cross that."

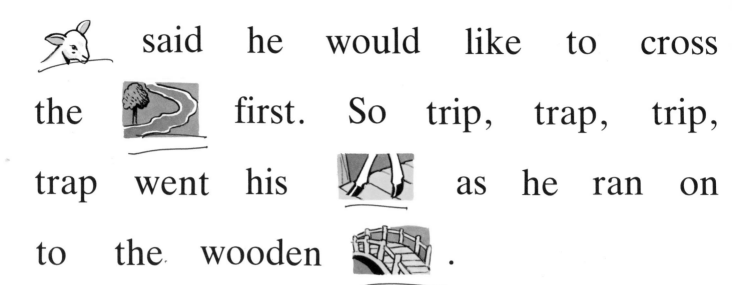 said he would like to cross the  first. So trip, trap, trip, trap went his  as he ran on to the wooden  .

Now under this 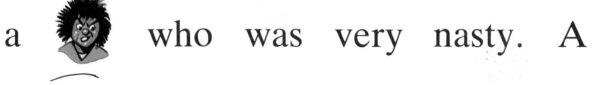 there lived

a  who was very nasty. A

is a big, bad goblin and this one

was very big and bad indeed.

Whenever he heard steps on the

he shouted, "Keep away or

I'll gobble you up!" So no one had

tried to cross the for years.

But now, here was  happily trip, trapping across the . As soon as the  heard him he shouted, "I'll gobble you up."

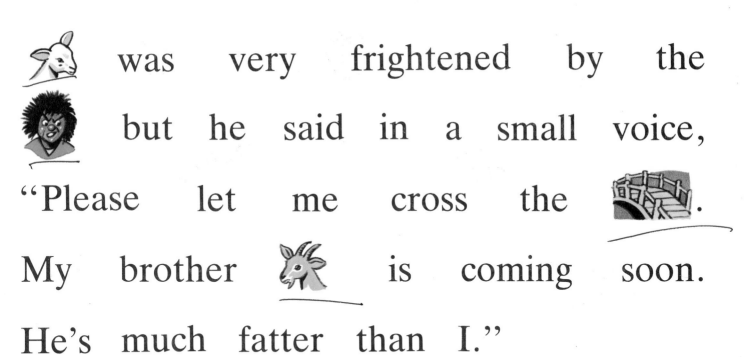 was very frightened by the but he said in a small voice, "Please let me cross the . My brother is coming soon. He's much fatter than I."

So the greedy  let 🐐 cross over the 🌉 to the 🌲 beyond. People who lived in the 🏠 on the hills above were amazed. It was their 🌉. They had built it. But no one had crossed it since the 👹 came to live beneath it.

No one had dared to cross the  since then. were warned, "Don't cross it to fly your on the hills beyond the ."

The  were told, "Don't cross the  to gather  in the . Keep away from the ."

So of course everyone was very surprised

to see  trotting over the .

Then as soon as he reached the ,

along came . Trip, trap, trip, trap

went his  as he ran onto the

wooden . "Keep off!" shouted

the , "or I'll gobble you up."

He looked so ugly  almost ran away.

But no, he stood firmly on the  instead and spoke softly to the . "Please don't gobble me up.  will be coming soon. There is more of him to eat."

So the  greedily said once more, "All right. I'll wait." And  crossed to the  and went skipping away with his little brother.

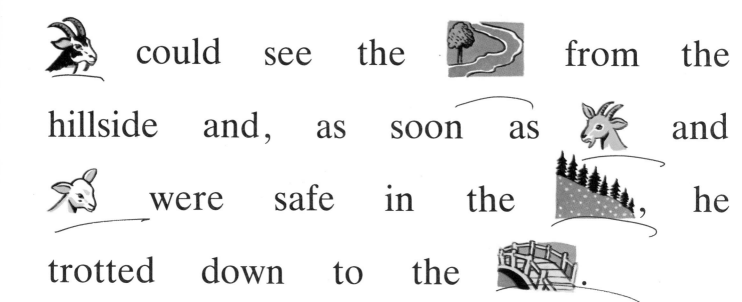

could see the 🌳🏞️ from the hillside and, as soon as 🐐 and 🐑 were safe in the 🌲⛰️, he trotted down to the 🌉.

Trip, trap, trip, trap, went his  as he ran on to the . When the saw him he shouted, "I'm going to gobble you up."

 snorted and stamped and bellowed, "You just try!" Then he lowered his  and Thump! He butted the  right off the .

Away went the  falling down, down to the ⬛. He disappeared into the deep 〰️ and no one ever saw him again.

 and  were jumping for joy in the . They ran down to meet  as he trotted over the . "We knew you could beat that ," they said.

Then the people came out of the

 on the hills and ran to the

 too. They could cross the

as much as they liked now. There

was no horrid  to stop them.

They brought honey  for

to eat, and gave them juicy

and little cream cheeses.

The  and came to the and made chains of for , and everyone was happy.